fiction

fiction

ISBN 978-0-692-09510-2

insig
htco
nvic
tion

wisd
omc
oura
ge.

x

new

no more
hence
forward again
yet
back. forward. back .back

here
and
again
we sink. sit .
sullen
forged

mystic
shining
laughter . smile. cheer
familiar
matching.
every . hope . again.

maybe

pretty
massive bail . treating
all
alike
less.more
none

but . this //.

something again/amiss
sing
treaty
for
fortune

my

nothing

many times ago, sat near a caustic
figure. transplanted with my memories
to tell, seek, comisserate . harrowing
down and through and under. casting the guise,
a figurehead of calm. metallic poise

against the masquerade. triumph . defeat.
simple.

echo

clever never once,
but twice.
simple
ignoring the best part.
simple severed signs
but obvious
cute
adored. finally
neat little books
adulating.
overly cautious
made
now knowing dealt
fortuitious
guiding blindly
without.

am biguity
,Through th e shadowy
lighte ned gla ss
,With subtle, memoirsin.
different

Ou t burst s
Control l ed sing;le
Every word.

With eve ryKisstou_chCaress a nd
E ver ylittlethin g ,youb reak
me again.
.ple asebr
eakmeagain.

f u
c k
 i n   g
g e
n i
 u s

stolen   hearts   jubilation
pounds
cat
ch.al.lt   hat
fuc
khe   l)the(l   star
tup
a   gain
thelit   tle
ge n   erat
ion,s   cy.
cles

Simple ,[though]
thoughts
,thinking every likeness
of control
[caused ,though
unintentional]
,fallingsimple.
[simple]fall.
sorry ;though
fact beholds
,i^could never
unintentionally
fallensimply
without. .

clever routes the course with not ches ab ove th e
dreary batthered path. brid ges. fog. awashed til
dragging and scream i ng and a llthosethings
t hat fade adjourn. simple. hidden. th ose
graceful glan ces. unseen. p erf ect. s ubtle
hints at the moon, the start, align please.just
a little can't seem to little bargain
for the matches, lightening the fray. tangled yet both
ob sessive mighty figurines. on display, on the
ground. en gulfed. estranged. for those and a
pint. a gain. chance happen. fort uitous. mystique
measured calculated trial. but why where how
wh en the who doesn't matter. still losing. for
everything that lost in love and lust and hoping
dig. deeper. depth. unearthed the tattered little
soul. the eyes. and hair and face. beaten. sold. fair
lost mystery. thought forced and drugged. not. fair. not
far above beneath lingering longing. not fair. not

wild

thorough . rough.

and through

magic

x

forced
time
away

passive . along the great wide waste
withal the ignored
troubles . riddle . past
mind your
own
dumb. deafening. turbulent .

queries. subtle . brash
and through

slack

waiting . waiting

simple. missing.

forced and troubled

funny it goes.

it
goes.

intent.

with time and subtle glances /
with stand . forget .doubt. thieves
mired , coursing through and over
yet over again. super freed.
not free. caught cable. wired
and forced. single, double . near
and then . . then

dream

never. fear

holding on, dreaming fiercely
daring
won't try
figuring
estimating
difficult, too different
please
let it go .definitely
fighting
chance doesn't stop
stop
you are not you
be
you just you
don't
want such obviousness
tragedy
just like me
dreamer
reminiscent of times
romantic
cannot be denied
stubborn
I'm so sorry, dear.

wa

it,dear love

tran sofrm a

gainin.to thel

i vingwish.ple

as eol vem

e dea rdo. a

gai

n elvo.,ou

.me

x

the along. thethe way
anyone could possibly know
however difficult. cruel.

decision. possible.   sly. stunt.

to the mountains. smile. wit. indelibly

asked
relented

up

once more. then twice

reality

know. travel. along

a grand work
of
fiction

star
tthinki
n

get
humor
                great
we
we
you

brutal
art
ownership
enough
impact

something someone
well
care and falseness

near . for . been
and
different misses

for been .meek

still. don't

collide without flying
vagabond for,all
triumphs. Where fair
mire pays too little
beauty overwhelmed. these
collisions often in
themselves too
in other.s
reality.must infusions
bitterness seek .dwell
among joy
no. the most
miniscule joy.s
interwoven into
tangled web of. off
why, , can
trials result.by
indifferent collisions lose,
at.least, sting,that
overwrought sense
interpretation falsely..

of   unretractable confusion
whether   improper
      untimely, all   to continue
prevail   impeccably unhear ever
unbearably truthful

hope levy
ing

dnt
leave

lost
ssing lo
to

h[,]me
aagin
gnissim
uoy
mi

ve

lucid

spectacular forgone

away

for you, Once aga in

Regardless of time or subtle   fears
cause   on my part, spite of   these

              stu b   born
I'm s o   s orry, de ar.

www.ingramcontent.com/pod-product-compliance
Lightning Source LLC
Chambersburg PA
CBHW061344040426
42444CB00011B/3078
* 9 7 8 0 6 9 2 0 9 5 1 0 2 *